MW00903724

HONOR

The Building Blocks of Honor for Hard Times: Bringing Meaning to Life – A Practical Guide for Young Adult Readers (12-18)

by Salvador Monastra-Sebasco

INSPIRING LANGUAGE PUBLISHING
O G D E N

Dedication

This syllabus is a guide to help you embark on a journey of self-discovery and resilience. At the heart of this book lies a roadmap designed to empower you through honor, dignity, and meaningful choices. By exploring the building blocks of honor, you'll gain the tools to navigate life's challenges, rebuild your strength, and embrace your true potential. Whether you are seeking guidance in hard times or striving to build a life of purpose, the lessons ahead offer a path forward in today's complex world. We hope this book serves as both a companion and a guide as you shape your own journey.

Syllabus for

The Building Blocks of Honor for Hard Times: Bringing Meaning to Life - **A Practical Guide for Young Adult Readers (12-18)**

Introduction: A Path Forward in a Changing World

- **Purpose:** To introduce the core idea of the book: discovering the power of honor, dignity, and meaningful choices in navigating life's challenges.

- **Key Themes:**

    - Why many young people feel lost or uncertain in today's world.

    - How this book offers a roadmap for reclaiming control over life and relationships.

    - The importance of finding personal purpose amidst the chaos.

Chapter 1: Understanding Honor in Today's World

- **Objective:** To introduce the concept of honor and its importance in modern life.

- **Key Themes:**

    - What is honor and why does it matter in our relationships and daily choices?

    - The role of honor in rebuilding dignity and self-respect.

    - How honor connects to personal power and meaning in tough times.

- **Exercises:**

    - Reflect on a time when you felt respected or disrespected. How did it affect your behavior and decisions?

Chapter 2: The Six Building Blocks of Honor

- **Objective:** To introduce the six core building blocks of honor: Faith, Presence, Significance, Identity, Choices, and Attention.

- **Key Themes:**
  - Understanding each building block and its role in creating a balanced and meaningful life.
  - Exploring how these blocks can be applied in everyday situations.
- **Exercises:**
  - Identify and write about which building block feels most relevant to you right now.

Chapter 3: Faith - Trusting in Yourself and the Process

- **Objective:** To explore the importance of faith in rebuilding strength and resilience.
- **Key Themes:**
  - What is faith beyond religion? How does faith in yourself and the world around you empower you to face challenges?
  - How to build faith in your own abilities and the choices you make.
- **Exercises:**
  - Write a letter to your future self, describing the strength and faith you will build in the coming months.

Chapter 4: Presence - Being Here, Now

- **Objective:** To learn the power of being present in your own life.
- **Key Themes:**
  - The role of presence in dealing with stress, uncertainty, and overwhelming emotions.
  - How to cultivate mindfulness and engage fully with the present moment.
- **Exercises:**
  - Practice mindfulness techniques for 5 minutes daily and reflect on your experience.

Chapter 5: Significance - Understanding Your Worth

- **Objective:** To help young adults reconnect with their sense of significance and self-worth.
- **Key Themes:**
  - Why recognizing your own value is crucial to building healthy relationships.
  - The impact of acknowledging your worth on how you interact with others and the choices you make.
- **Exercises:**

- Write a list of qualities or achievements that make you proud of yourself.

Chapter 6: Identity - Embracing Who You Are

- **Objective:** To explore the process of understanding and accepting your identity.
- **Key Themes:**
  - The importance of knowing who you are in a world that often feels full of expectations.
  - How your identity influences your relationships, decisions, and personal goals.
- **Exercises:**
  - Create a visual representation (drawing, collage, or journal entry) of your identity, highlighting what makes you unique.

Chapter 7: Choices - Empowering Yourself Through Decisions

- **Objective:** To emphasize the power of choice in shaping your life.
- **Key Themes:**
  - How your choices define your path and how to make decisions with intention and confidence.
  - Understanding that, even in hard times, you have control over your responses and actions.
- **Exercises:**
  - Reflect on a recent decision you made. What were the consequences, and what would you change, if anything?

Chapter 8: Attention - The Power of Focus

- **Objective:** To explore the role of attention in creating meaningful experiences.
- **Key Themes:**
  - How paying attention to the right things can guide your relationships, choices, and personal growth.
  - The effects of distractions and how to improve focus on what truly matters.
- **Exercises:**
  - Practice focusing on one task without distractions for 10 minutes. Journal your thoughts on the experience.

Chapter 9: Building Meaningful Relationships

- **Objective:** To teach young adults how to apply the building blocks of honor in their relationships with others.
- **Key Themes:**
    - The importance of mutual respect, trust, and understanding in building lasting friendships and connections.
    - How to use the building blocks to improve communication and conflict resolution.
- **Exercises:**
    - Have a conversation with a close friend or family member using the principles of honor you've learned.

Chapter 10: Navigating Hard Times with Honor

- **Objective:** To provide practical advice for using the building blocks of honor to cope with life's toughest moments.
- **Key Themes:**
    - How to maintain dignity and self-respect when facing difficult situations.
    - The power of resilience and the ability to rebuild your life after setbacks.
- **Exercises:**
    - Reflect on a difficult time in your life. How did you handle it? How could you have used the building blocks of honor to navigate it differently?

Chapter 11: Moving Forward: Living with Purpose and Integrity

- **Objective:** To encourage young adults to continue applying the principles of honor in their everyday lives for ongoing growth and success.
- **Key Themes:**
    - How to maintain focus on what truly matters, even as life changes.
    - Setting goals based on your values and building a future that reflects who you are.
- **Exercises:**
    - Create a vision board or goal-setting list that incorporates your core values and the building blocks of honor.

Conclusion: The Power of Honor in Action

- **Objective:** To wrap up the key lessons from the book and inspire young readers to continue their journey of self-discovery.

- **Key Themes:**
    - The importance of continuing to practice honor, resilience, and self-awareness.
    - How the building blocks of honor can transform your life and relationships, no matter where you start.

- **Exercises:**
    - Write a letter to your future self about the changes you've made and the path you want to continue on.

Additional Resources

- **Suggested Reading:** A list of books, articles, and podcasts for further exploration of personal development, mindfulness, and relationship building.

- **Support Networks:** Information on how to find mentors, counselors, and other supportive resources for personal growth.

This syllabus offers a roadmap for young adults to navigate the complexities of life by focusing on personal growth, dignity, and the choices they make. By providing practical advice and exercises, it ensures that readers have the tools to rebuild strength, purpose, and meaningful relationships, empowering them to face the challenges of their journey with confidence and resilience.

Introduction: A Path Forward in a Changing World

When I set out to write *The Building Blocks of Honor for Hard Times: Bringing Meaning to Life*, I couldn't shake the idea that honor could be the key to surviving the toughest moments in life. It's a concept we often overlook, but it holds the power to help us reclaim control, find meaning, and rediscover purpose in an uncertain world.

In today's world, it's easy to feel lost. Everywhere we look, we see chaos, confusion, and division. It feels like the ground beneath us is constantly shifting, and it's difficult to know where we stand. Maybe you've felt disconnected from what really matters, or overwhelmed by the pressures of society, social media, or expectations from others. The constant change, combined with the loss of clarity, can make it seem like we're just drifting without a clear sense of direction.

But here's the truth: when we learn to understand and embrace honor, we can start rebuilding our lives. Honor isn't just a word or abstract concept—it's the foundation of dignity, respect, and meaningful relationships. It's a bridge that connects the chaos around us to the calm within us. And it's through honor that we can restore balance, even in the most challenging times.

Too often, we hear about division and heartache in the world, caused by a lack of respect—not just towards others, but also towards ourselves.

Honor isn't about seeking recognition or praise from others. It's about how we show up in the world, how we treat each other, and most importantly, how we make choices that reflect our values.

Honor isn't about perfection—it's about integrity, the small actions we take that add up to something meaningful.

This book isn't just a list of rules or superficial advice. It's a guide for real transformation, a way to build inner strength and resilience that helps you make better choices, rebuild relationships, and navigate tough times with dignity.

The Building Blocks of Honor for Hard Times isn't theoretical—it's practical, offering you tools to change your life right now, no matter what challenges you face.

Through this book, you'll learn how to:

- **Rebuild your sense of self-worth**, not by what you own or what others think of you, but by what you stand for and the integrity you embody every day.
- **Create meaningful connections in your relationships**, focusing on depth and respect rather than surface-level interactions and fleeting moments.
- **Understand love as something lasting**, rooted in mutual respect and honor, rather than as something temporary or transactional.

The six building blocks—Faith, Presence, Significance, Identity, Choices, and Attention—are your roadmap to reclaiming meaning, direction, and strength in a world that often feels overwhelming and unpredictable.

These aren't just abstract ideas; they are actionable steps to bring order to the chaos and restore balance in your life.

This book isn't about waiting for the world to change—it's about learning how to change your response to the world. It's about learning how to take control, lead by example, and create a space of respect and dignity for yourself and those around you.

Whether you're struggling personally or simply watching the world shift around you, this book will show you that you don't have to feel powerless. Honor is something you can tap into right now, and it has the power to transform not only your life but also the lives of those you care about.

The Building Blocks of Honor for Hard Times will help you discover how to bring meaning, peace, and lasting change into your life—no matter how turbulent the world around you may seem.

In a world full of uncertainty, it's time to find your path forward—and honor will show you the way.

Chapter 1: Understanding Honor in Today's World

In a world that seems dominated by constant change, chaos often feels like the only thing we can rely on. From global unrest to personal struggles, it's easy to feel disconnected, uncertain, and powerless. In moments of confusion and frustration, it's difficult to find a sense of direction, let alone a path forward.

Yet, despite the chaos that surrounds us, one powerful truth remains: honor is the key to navigating these turbulent times. But honor isn't about accolades or public recognition; it's something far deeper. Honor is the core of dignity, respect, and meaningful relationships, and it's more relevant now than ever.

At its core, honor is about understanding and honoring our own worth, as well as the worth of others. It shapes how we treat ourselves, how we interact with others, and how we live in a way that reflects our true values. In a world that often feels fractured, honor is the glue that holds everything together.

We see the consequences of a lack of honor in today's society everywhere.

From the breakdown of trust between individuals to the erosion of respect in communities and workplaces, the absence of honor is a driving force behind division, conflict, and confusion.

Whether it's through subtle disregard for others' dignity or outright division, when honor is lost, we feel disconnected and adrift.

The good news is that honor is something we can rebuild. It's not a distant or idealistic concept—it's a practice. It's a choice to engage meaningfully with the world around us, to show respect and care for others, and to rebuild the connections that matter.

Honor is something we create, moment by moment, choice by choice.

In this chapter, we'll explore how honor can be the anchor that keeps us grounded, no matter how chaotic life may seem.

When we choose to act with honor, we not only elevate our own lives, but we also contribute to an environment where those around us can thrive. Honor is the foundation of strong relationships, empowered choices, and a life lived with integrity and purpose. It gives us the strength to stand firm, even when the world around us feels uncertain.

What Does Honor Really Mean?

Honor often gets misunderstood as something reserved for special occasions or for those who are famous or influential. But true honor isn't about status—it's about the deep respect we show ourselves and others. It's about acknowledging the inherent worth of every person, regardless of their background or circumstances.

Honor is more than just being polite or acting with good manners. It's about valuing people for who they are, not just for what they can do for us. It's about treating people with dignity, even when we don't agree with them, even when they've hurt us, or when they've made mistakes. It's about seeing the humanity in others, and recognizing that everyone has a unique story, a unique worth, and a unique set of experiences.

This chapter redefines honor as an active choice. It's not something that happens automatically—it's something we consciously choose every day, in every interaction, in every decision. It's how we show up in the world, how we make choices that align with our deepest values, and how we live with integrity even when no one is watching.

Honor isn't an abstract idea—it's a way of life that has the power to transform relationships, communities, and even entire societies. It's a small act of kindness, a deep respect for others' opinions, and a commitment to doing what's right, no matter how difficult the situation may be.

Honor in Action

To understand the power of honor, it's helpful to think of someone you admire—a person whose actions inspire you. Chances are, this person has a deep understanding of honor. They act with integrity, and their choices reflect their commitment to dignity and respect. This person has mastered the art of showing up with honor in every aspect of their life.

Honor isn't just about big, grand gestures. It shows up in the small moments—the way we listen, the way we communicate, the way we treat others with kindness, even when they may not deserve it. It's present in how we handle conflict, in the decisions we make when no one is watching, and in how we respect others, especially when we don't agree.

Honor is like an energy—it ripples through everything we do. When we act with honor, we create an environment where trust, respect, and collaboration flourish. And when we lead with honor, we set an example for others to follow. Honor is contagious. It spreads from one person to another, and before long, it can transform a whole community.

The Six Building Blocks of Honor

So, how do we begin to build a life of honor? Understanding what honor is is just the first step. To truly embody honor in our lives, we need to practice it every day. That's where the six building blocks of honor come in.

These six principles are foundational to living a life of meaning, integrity, and purpose.

1. **Faith**: Not necessarily religious faith, but the belief in something greater than ourselves—an understanding that we are part of something bigger and more meaningful.

2. **Presence**: Being fully engaged in the moment, giving others our full attention, and being present for those we care about, without distractions.

3. **Significance**: Recognizing our inherent worth and the value of every person we encounter, understanding that our actions have a ripple effect on the world around us.

4. **Identity**: Knowing who we are, what we stand for, and how we make choices that align with our values, so we can show up confidently in every situation.

5. **Choices**: Understanding that every decision, big or small, shapes the world around us. Honor is reflected in the choices we make and how those choices align with our core values.

6. **Attention**: Giving our full attention to what matters most, whether it's a relationship, a task, or a personal growth journey, without shortcuts or distractions.

Each of these building blocks is essential to creating a life that reflects honor and meaning, even when the world around us feels chaotic. Together, they create a strong foundation that can help us navigate the toughest challenges and rebuild what's been lost.

Why Honor Matters More Than Ever

In a world that often feels divided and disconnected, honor offers us a path forward. It reminds us of the shared humanity that unites us all. Honor is about more than just personal success or individual happiness; it's about creating a world where everyone can thrive. It's about relationships, respect, and making choices that benefit the greater good.

As you continue reading, you'll explore how each of these six building blocks of honor can help you bring more meaning, purpose, and integrity into your life.

You'll learn how to incorporate these principles into your daily actions and choices, transforming not just your life but also the lives of those around you.

The journey toward a life of honor begins here, with the understanding that honor isn't just an ideal—it's a practical tool that can help you find direction, rebuild connections, and create lasting change. By embracing honor, you're taking the first step toward a more fulfilling, connected, and purposeful life.

Exercises:

- Reflect on a time when you felt respected or disrespected. How did it affect your behavior and decisions?

Chapter 2: The Six Building Blocks of Honor

In a world that seems to shift beneath our feet, where values often feel relative and chaos is omnipresent, the search for meaning becomes even more urgent. From societal instability to personal turmoil, it is easy to lose sight of what truly matters.

Yet, in these turbulent times, there is one timeless principle that stands strong and offers clarity: honor.

But honor is not a distant, abstract concept reserved for the few or the ancient.

It is alive today, deeply relevant, and within our reach. Honor provides a moral compass that can guide us through the chaos of life, helping us to define not only who we are but how we interact with others and the world around us.

To harness the power of honor, however, we need to understand its foundations—its building blocks. These six essential elements of honor form the framework upon which we can build a meaningful, authentic life.

The Importance of Honor in Today's World

In our current climate, characterized by divisive opinions, social pressures, and an overwhelming emphasis on external validation, honor can feel like an elusive and outdated notion. Social media constantly bombards us with messages about "success," often measured by followers, likes, and material accomplishments. We find ourselves comparing, competing, and striving to "win" at life, often at the expense of our true selves. In this noise, we can lose track of what truly matters.

Honor, however, transcends superficial metrics of success. It is not about external praise or recognition. Honor is rooted in self-respect and respect for others. It is about making choices that reflect our values and living in alignment with the highest standards of integrity. Honor is not a fleeting concept, but a timeless principle that grounds us in our relationships, decisions, and interactions.

In a world that feels increasingly fragmented, honor has the potential to unite us. It is a principle that can bridge gaps between cultures, ideologies, and individuals. Honor brings us back to what is essential—love, respect, integrity, and connection. It's not about conforming to someone else's idea of success, but about embracing our authentic selves and fostering meaningful relationships.

The Six Elements of Honor

To fully embrace the power of honor, we must cultivate the six building blocks that serve as its foundation. These elements are more than just philosophical ideas; they are actionable principles that guide how we live, how we treat others, and how we define our identity.

The first and perhaps most important step in living with honor is recognizing who you truly are—your independent identity. In today's world, there is immense pressure to conform, to measure our worth against others' expectations, or to adopt identities shaped by external achievements.

However, honor begins by acknowledging that your true value is not defined by societal standards, titles, or fleeting accomplishments. Your worth is inherent, and it is not contingent upon meeting others' expectations.

In the journey of personal growth, especially as young adults navigating new phases of life, the question of "Who am I?" often feels daunting. We may find ourselves searching for identity in our grades, career choices, or even the approval of others.

However, honor teaches us to look inward—to understand that who we are at our core is enough. We don't need to become someone else or fit a mold. Instead, we are encouraged to embrace our authentic selves, shaped by our beliefs, values, and experiences.

Recognizing your authenticity means rejecting the notion that your worth is determined by what you do or what others think of you.

Honor teaches us to honor our individuality—not just in theory, but in practice. This recognition of our own identity paves the way for honoring others in the same way. True honor respects people for who they are, not for what they can offer or how they align with our personal expectations.

When we recognize our own worth and honor ourselves, it becomes much easier to honor others. This recognition is the beginning of a healthy cycle of respect, where self-respect fosters respect for others, and respect for others in turn deepens our understanding of our own value.

The Journey of Self-Discovery

Recognizing your authenticity is not a one-time achievement but an ongoing process. It involves continuously reflecting on who you are beneath external labels and expectations. Who are you when no one is watching? What values guide your actions, regardless of the opinions of others?

This journey is crucial, especially in a world where identities are often shaped by external forces. As we grow, we must learn to strip away societal labels and understand our true selves. This self-awareness enables us to act with integrity, make decisions aligned with our values, and engage in relationships that honor our true identity.

But how do we know what self-awareness is unless we know what the meaning of the word self is? SELF is a PRESENCE OF EXISTENCE.

Take a moment to reflect on your own journey of self-discovery. When have you felt most aligned with your values? When have you acted with honor, not for recognition but simply because it was the right thing to do? Honor does not ask for perfection—it asks for self-acceptance and continuous growth.

We are all flawed, and part of each our own authenticity is embracing these imperfections, while striving to live with integrity.

Taking Responsibility for Your Actions

Another critical aspect of your authenticity is taking responsibility for your actions. As you transition into adulthood, you begin to make decisions that will impact your future—decisions related to your career, relationships, and personal growth.

Honor requires you to take ownership of these decisions and their consequences. It is easy to act impulsively or shift blame, but true honor means being accountable for your choices.

Taking responsibility means understanding that your actions don't exist in a vacuum. Every choice you make affects others, whether directly or indirectly.

By taking responsibility for our actions, we ensure that we are building a foundation of trust and integrity with others. These small, everyday decisions reflect our commitment to living with honor.

The Power of Reflection

The practice of reflection is vital in the journey toward recognizing and honoring your authenticity.

It is in moments of quiet introspection that we learn who we are and why we act the way we do. Reflection helps us assess whether our actions align with our true values and whether we are living with integrity.

In this chapter, I encourage you to engage in SELF-reflection. Consider: What does your authenticity look like? How have you honored yourself in the past, and how can you honor yourself moving forward? Reflecting on your authenticity and your actions will empower you to make intentional choices that align with the honor you wish to cultivate in your life.

As we continue in this book, we will explore the six building blocks of honor, each offering powerful tools for living a purposeful and meaningful life. For now, focus on this new meaning of self. Embrace who you truly are, reflect on your journey, and take responsibility for your actions.

Honor begins with the SELF of you and from that foundation, you can build a life filled with integrity, respect, and connection.

In the next chapter, we will explore **Faith – Trusting in Yourself and the Process**, a crucial building block of honor, and examine how our attention can shape the world around us.

Remember, honor begins with you. By recognizing your worth and embracing your authenticity, you lay the groundwork for a life that honors both yourself and others. The journey toward a life of honor starts now, and it begins with you.

Exercises:

- Identify and write about which building block feels most relevant to you right now.

Chapter 3: Faith – Trusting in Yourself and the Process

In today's world, where uncertainty is a constant companion, one of the greatest challenges we face is trusting the journey we are on. From navigating personal struggles to grappling with external pressures, it's easy to feel lost and unsure of where we are headed. We often look for guarantees, clear directions, or immediate outcomes.

Yet, true success and growth in life require a different kind of trust—a deeper, more resilient faith in both ourselves and the process we're experiencing.

Faith isn't just about religious beliefs or waiting for something external to change. It's about an internal conviction that we are capable of overcoming challenges and achieving meaningful growth, even when the path isn't clear. It's about trusting that, even in the face of uncertainty, we can rise to the occasion, learn from our experiences, and move forward with confidence.

This chapter will explore how faith—faith in yourself, in others, and in the process of life—can transform your ability to live with honor and navigate life's inevitable challenges.

The Importance of Faith in Today's World

In a world dominated by instant gratification, we often forget that lasting progress takes time. Whether it's personal development, career growth, or meaningful relationships, the process is rarely linear or predictable. But this does not mean that we should lose trust in the journey.

Faith in today's context is not about blind hope or expecting everything to work out without effort. It is the belief that you have the strength, resilience, and guidance necessary to navigate life, no matter how difficult or uncertain the road ahead may seem. When we lack that result of faith—whether in ourselves or in the world around us—we become paralyzed by fear, self-doubt, and impatience.

We may feel as though we are stuck or that we will never achieve our goals. But true faith allows us to embrace the unknown with courage and patience, knowing that growth often comes from unexpected places and through unforeseen challenges.

Faith teaches us to trust the process—not just the end result. It reminds us that every step, even the setbacks, has value.

The lessons learned in times of struggle shape us and prepare us for future success. In essence, faith in yourself is an investment in your future growth, even when the outcomes are not immediately visible.

Faith in Yourself: Building Inner Confidence

The first and most important place to start is with faith in yourself. Without this, all other forms of faith will be built on shaky ground. Trusting in your own abilities, wisdom, and judgment is the foundation for creating a life of honor.

Self-doubt is a powerful force—it can hold you back, keep you small, and make you second-guess every decision you make. However, when you develop faith in yourself, you tap into a wellspring of resilience and clarity.

Faith in yourself is not about perfection or having all the answers. It is about believing that, even if you don't have it all figured out right now, you are capable of learning, adapting, and moving forward.

You trust in your ability to make choices aligned with your values, even when the path forward is unclear.

This faith empowers you to take action, make decisions, and trust the process, knowing that your choices are leading you toward growth and greater self-awareness.

The more you practice trusting yourself, the stronger this inner faith becomes. It becomes a cycle—taking action builds trust, and trust leads to more decisive and aligned actions.

Faith in the Process: Embracing the Journey

Once you've begun to trust yourself, the next step is to trust the process—the unfolding journey of life. Faith in the process means acknowledging that growth happens over time, and that the road to success is rarely straight or predictable.

It means understanding that every experience—good or bad—is part of a larger story, and that setbacks and failures are not signs of defeat, but opportunities for learning and growth.

When we lack faith in the process, we can become impatient and frustrated. We want quick results, immediate success, or external validation. However, the most meaningful outcomes in life rarely come quickly or easily.

Trusting the process is about letting go of the need to control every aspect of your journey and surrendering to the lessons and challenges that come your way.

This kind of faith enables us to be patient with ourselves and with others, even in the face of uncertainty. It teaches us to remain grounded, even when the future feels unpredictable. Faith in the process also means having the courage to stay on course when things don't unfold as planned. It's about understanding that setbacks are not failures, but necessary parts of the journey. Life's process is not about perfection—it's about evolution, growth, and refinement.

Overcoming Doubt: The Role of Faith in Building Resilience

One of the most powerful ways faith manifests in our lives is in its ability to build resilience. Life is full of obstacles, challenges, and moments when we feel overwhelmed. In these moments, doubt often creeps in, and we may question whether we're on the right path or if we're good enough to succeed.

Faith provides us with the strength to push through these moments of doubt. It helps us see beyond our current circumstances and trust that, if we keep moving forward, we will grow and emerge stronger.

Resilience is not about never facing difficulty, but about having the faith to keep going in the face of adversity. It is about trusting that, even when things seem impossible, we have the inner resources to find a way through.

Resilience, supported by faith, allows us to keep our eyes on the bigger picture, to remember that challenges are temporary, and that every step forward is a step toward greater wisdom and understanding.

The more you trust in yourself and in the process, the more resilient you become. And the more resilient you are, the more you are able to honor yourself and others, because you understand the power of perseverance and the value of growth through struggle.

Practical Steps to Cultivate Faith

Faith is not something that magically appears; it is something we must actively cultivate. Here are a few practical steps to help you build and strengthen your faith in yourself and in the process:

1. **Practice Self-Affirmation**: Start by affirming your worth and your capabilities. Remind yourself daily of your strengths, your values, and your potential. When doubt arises, counter it with affirmations that remind you of the progress you've made and your ability to handle challenges.

2. **Embrace the Journey**: Trust that every experience is part of your personal growth. Even the difficult moments are shaping you into the person you are meant to become. Instead of focusing solely on the outcome, appreciate the lessons and growth along the way.

3. **Let Go of Perfection**: Faith isn't about perfection—it's about progress. Release the need to control everything and accept that mistakes, setbacks, and failures are all part of the process. Trust that you are evolving with each step you take.

4. **Build Resilience**: Resilience is born from faith. The next time you face a challenge, pause and remind yourself that you can navigate through it. Trust that you have the inner strength to handle whatever comes your way.

5. **Celebrate Small Wins**: Recognize and celebrate the small victories along the journey. Each step forward, no matter how small, is a testament to your growth and faith in the process.

Why Faith Matters More Than Ever

In a world that often values quick success and immediate gratification, faith may seem like a slow, invisible force. But it is precisely in times of uncertainty and chaos that faith becomes an anchor, providing us with the strength to move forward with purpose. Faith in yourself and in the process is not only essential for personal growth, but it is also the cornerstone of living with honor.

When you trust yourself and the journey, you begin to make decisions with confidence, honor your values, and remain grounded despite external chaos. This kind of faith transforms how you approach challenges, relationships, and your future. It allows you to create a life that is not only successful, but deeply meaningful.

In the next chapter, we will explore **Presence**—how being fully engaged in the present moment deepens your connection to yourself, to others, and to the process of life. The journey continues, and with faith as your guide, you are prepared to face whatever comes your way with courage and integrity.

Faith starts with you. Trust in your ability, trust in the process, and honor yourself and the journey you are on.

Exercises:
- Write a letter to your future self, describing the strength and faith you will build in the coming months

Chapter 4: Presence – Being Here, Now

In our fast-paced, distraction-filled world, being fully present often feels like an elusive goal. We are constantly pulled in multiple directions, juggling responsibilities, scrolling through social media, or worrying about the past and future.

Yet, the truth is that the key to living a life of honor and purpose lies in our ability to be present—truly engaged in the moment, right here, right now.

Presence is not simply about being physically in a place; it's about actively engaging with the world around you. It's about being mentally and emotionally available, focusing your attention on the task at hand, and immersing yourself in the present experience. Presence requires us to put aside distractions and fully commit to the moment, allowing us to connect with ourselves, others, and life itself in a deeper, more meaningful way.

In this chapter, we will explore what it means to be truly present, why it's essential for living with honor, and how cultivating presence can enhance every aspect of our lives.

The Importance of Presence in Today's World

In a world full of noise—where the next notification, meeting, or deadline is always around the corner—it's easy to overlook the power of presence. We may find ourselves thinking about what's next or replaying past events, leaving little room to experience the richness of the current moment. Yet, being present is a fundamental part of leading a life of honor.

When we're fully present, we honor ourselves and others by being mindful and attentive. Presence allows us to truly listen to people, connect authentically, and engage deeply with our work and relationships. It is through presence that we show our respect for the time and energy others are giving us, and we demonstrate our commitment to living with integrity and focus.

Moreover, presence is essential for our mental and emotional well-being. When we are present, we reduce stress, anxiety, and overwhelm, because we stop worrying about what we cannot control.

Instead, we ground ourselves in the reality of the here and now, where we have the power to make decisions and take action. Presence gives us the clarity to focus on what truly matters, rather than being swept away by the external noise or internal distractions.

Being Present with Yourself

The foundation of presence starts with being present with yourself. How often do you find yourself rushing from one task to the next, without taking a moment to check in with yourself? How often do you sit with your thoughts, your emotions, or your body without distraction? The first step in cultivating presence is learning how to be with yourself in a meaningful way.

When you are present with yourself, you honor your own needs and desires. You listen to your body, understand your emotions, and give yourself the time and space to reflect. Being present with yourself allows you to connect with your deeper sense of purpose and values, ensuring that your actions are aligned with who you truly are.

One of the most powerful ways to practice being present with yourself is through mindfulness. Mindfulness is the practice of paying attention to the present moment without judgment.

It involves observing your thoughts, feelings, and physical sensations with curiosity and acceptance, rather than reacting to them impulsively. By practicing mindfulness, you begin to cultivate a deeper awareness of your inner world, which helps you make decisions with clarity and integrity.

Being Present with Others

Another essential aspect of presence is being fully present with others. In our relationships, how often do we find ourselves distracted—checking our phones during conversations, thinking about what we're going to say next, or mentally preparing for the next task? True presence with others means offering your full attention and engaging with them on a deeper level.

When we are present with others, we demonstrate respect and honor. We show that we value their time, emotions, and thoughts. This level of presence fosters connection, trust, and empathy in our relationships.

People can sense when we are truly listening, when we are engaged in the conversation, and when we are there for them—not just physically, but mentally and emotionally.

Being present with others also allows us to build stronger, more meaningful relationships.

We become better listeners, more compassionate friends, partners, and family members. We are able to support others in a way that feels authentic and grounded. Presence strengthens the bonds between us and creates an environment where mutual respect and understanding can flourish.

The Power of Attention

At the core of presence lies the power of attention. Attention is a valuable resource in today's world—one that is constantly being pulled in different directions.

However, attention is also the gateway to connection and growth. When we direct our attention toward something, we bring our full energy and focus to it, elevating its importance in our lives.

Attention is a form of honor. When we give our attention to someone or something, we are saying, "You matter. This moment matters." Whether we are working, talking to a loved one, or enjoying a hobby, our attention shows our commitment to the present experience.

In today's world, where distractions are endless, attention is a powerful tool that can help us stay grounded and focused on what truly matters.

To cultivate presence, we must learn to direct our attention deliberately.

This means putting away distractions, slowing down, and choosing to engage fully in whatever we are doing. It could be as simple as listening attentively to a friend, focusing on a task at work, or taking a moment to appreciate the beauty of nature.

The more we practice directing our attention in meaningful ways, the more present we become in every area of our lives.

Overcoming Distractions and Finding Focus

One of the biggest challenges in cultivating presence is overcoming the distractions that constantly compete for our attention.

From social media notifications to the pressure of multitasking, it can feel impossible to stay focused on the present moment. Yet, in order to live with honor and integrity, we must learn to manage these distractions and create space for presence.

One way to overcome distractions is to set boundaries. This could mean setting specific times for checking emails or social media, or creating designated periods of time where you focus solely on one task. By setting these boundaries, you allow yourself to be fully present in the moments that matter most.

Another powerful tool for overcoming distractions is practicing mindfulness techniques such as deep breathing, meditation, or body awareness.

These practices help center your attention, calm your mind, and refocus your energy on the present moment. The more you practice mindfulness, the easier it becomes to tune out distractions and stay present in your life.

Presence and Honor: A Deep Connection

Being present is not only a tool for personal growth and well-being; it is also a key component of living with honor. Honor is about giving respect to yourself and others, and presence is a direct expression of that respect.

When you are present, you demonstrate that you value the time and energy of those around you, and that you are committed to living with integrity in every moment.

Honor, in its truest sense, is about being mindful and intentional in how we show up in the world. It is about being present for ourselves, for others, and for the experiences that shape our lives.

When we are present, we are better equipped to make decisions aligned with our values, build deeper connections with others, and lead lives that reflect our true purpose.

Practical Steps to Cultivate Presence

1. **Practice Mindfulness**: Start by practicing mindfulness techniques, such as focusing on your breath or observing your thoughts without judgment. Begin with short sessions and gradually increase the time you spend in mindfulness practice.

2. **Set Boundaries for Distractions**: Identify the distractions that pull you away from the present moment and set boundaries for them. This could mean turning off notifications, limiting screen time, or creating designated spaces for focused work.

3. **Engage in Active Listening**: When interacting with others, focus entirely on what they are saying. Put away distractions, make eye contact, and listen with the intent to understand, not just to respond.

4. **Slow Down**: Take time to savor the moments of your day, whether it's enjoying a meal, taking a walk, or having a conversation. Slow down and allow yourself to fully experience these moments without rushing.

5. **Reflect Regularly**: Take time each day to reflect on your actions and experiences. What moments did you feel truly present? Where did you struggle with distractions? Reflection helps you refine your ability to be present over time.

Why Presence Matters More Than Ever

In a world where we are constantly pulled in different directions, presence is a rare and precious gift.

The gift we give is the life we live. It allows us to honor ourselves, our relationships, and the moments that make life meaningful. By cultivating presence, we create a foundation of connection, respect, and purpose in our lives. We step away from the noise and chaos and center ourselves in the here and now—where we have the power to create meaningful change.

In the next chapter, we will explore **Significance**—the power of understanding your worth and the impact of your actions. The journey of presence is just the beginning. As we continue, we will dive deeper into the core building blocks of honor that shape how we live and interact with the world.

Presence starts with you. Be here, now. Honor the moment, and honor yourself and those around you.

Exercises:

- Practice mindfulness techniques for 5 minutes daily and reflect on your experience.

Chapter 5: Significance – Understanding Your Worth

In a world that constantly measures success by external factors—money, status, accomplishments—it's easy to forget that true significance doesn't come from external validation. It's not about how many followers you have, how impressive your resume looks, or how much you achieve.

True significance is an internal recognition of your inherent worth, independent of anything you can accomplish or the titles you can claim. It is about understanding that who you are—your very existence—has meaning and value.

In this chapter, we will explore the concept of significance as it relates to your identity, purpose, and actions.

By understanding and embracing your own worth, you not only elevate your own life but also positively impact the world around you.

Recognizing your significance is crucial to living a life of honor because it empowers you to act with integrity, make choices aligned with your true values, and offer genuine respect to others.

The Search for Significance

In today's society, many people are caught up in the quest for significance by external means. We chase promotions, accolades, or material wealth, thinking that these accomplishments will make us feel valuable.

However, when we tie our worth to these fleeting measures of success, we can easily fall into the trap of feeling inadequate when we don't reach our goals or live up to other people's expectations.

But true significance comes from within. It's not about what you do or how others perceive you. It's about knowing that you have inherent value simply because you exist.

Understanding your worth is the first step toward living a life of purpose, direction, and honor.

The pressure to prove ourselves can be overwhelming, especially for young adults who are beginning to chart their path in the world. It's easy to compare ourselves to others, measuring our success against theirs and wondering why we haven't "made it" yet. The key to overcoming this pressure is to stop measuring your worth by external metrics and start embracing the deep, unshakable value that lies within you.

The Importance of Recognizing Your Own Worth

To live with honor, it's crucial that we first recognize our own significance. If we don't understand our worth, we are at risk of selling ourselves short—

settling for relationships, careers, and experiences that don't reflect who we truly are. When we acknowledge our inherent value, we empower ourselves to make choices that align with our best interests, purpose, and integrity.

Recognizing your worth is a radical act of self-love and self-respect. It's about acknowledging that you are deserving of kindness, success, and fulfillment, regardless of your past or what others think of you.

This doesn't mean you are perfect or free from mistakes; rather, it means that you honor yourself enough to believe that you have something of great value to offer the world.

When you truly recognize your worth, you begin to set healthier boundaries, make more confident decisions, and invest in relationships and endeavors that nurture your growth.. You stop seeking validation from others and start validating yourself. This internal recognition of your worth is the foundation for a life filled with honor, purpose, and fulfillment.

How Significance Shapes Your Actions

Understanding your significance doesn't just affect your sense of self—it also shapes the way you act in the world.

When you understand your own worth, you make decisions from a place of strength and clarity. You no longer allow the opinions of others or external circumstances to dictate how you behave. Instead, you make choices that reflect your values and your sense of what's truly important.

For example, when you understand your significance, you no longer settle for toxic relationships or environments that drain you. You seek out people and opportunities that uplift you and align with your authentic self. You begin to prioritize your well-being, your dreams, and your purpose over societal expectations or superficial desires.

Significance also informs the way you treat others. When you understand that you are worthy of respect, you are more likely to extend that same respect to others.

You see the value in every person you meet, regardless of their background, appearance, or status. By recognizing your own worth, you naturally begin to honor the worth of others, and this creates a ripple effect of respect, kindness, and connection.

The Role of Vulnerability in Embracing Your Significance

One of the greatest barriers to understanding our own significance is the fear of vulnerability.

We may be afraid that if we acknowledge our worth, we will be seen as arrogant or self-centered. Or, conversely, we may worry that others will not value us in the way we hope, leaving us feeling rejected or unimportant.

However, vulnerability is not a sign of weakness; it is a sign of courage. To fully embrace your significance, you must be willing to show up as your authentic self, without hiding or pretending. You must be willing to stand in your truth, knowing that your worth does not depend on the approval or validation of others.

When you allow yourself to be vulnerable, you open the door to deeper connections with others. You give yourself the freedom to live without the fear of judgment or failure. Yes, vulnerabilities are like street signs to your needs.

Embracing your vulnerability allows you to step into your full potential, knowing that your significance is not determined by perfection, but by your willingness to show up as you are.

The Power of Self-Acceptance

At the heart of understanding your significance is self-acceptance. It is the practice of acknowledging your flaws, mistakes, and imperfections while still recognizing that you are worthy of love, respect, and success.

Self-acceptance is a key component of building honor because it allows you to embrace your identity without shame or self-criticism.

When you accept yourself, you stop chasing the approval of others or trying to live up to unattainable standards. Instead, you find peace in who you are and what you bring to the world. You begin to honor yourself for all that you are—not just the parts that others deem valuable, but the whole, imperfect you.

Self-acceptance allows you to approach life with confidence and authenticity. You stop measuring your worth against external achievements or the opinions of others. Instead, you recognize that your significance is inherent and unshakable.

Practicing Significance in Everyday Life

Understanding your worth is not something that happens overnight—it's a practice that requires continual reflection and growth. Here are some ways to begin embracing your significance in everyday life:

1. **Practice Self-Compassion**: Be kind to yourself. Recognize when you're being too hard on yourself and offer yourself the same understanding and care that you would offer to a friend. Self-compassion is a powerful tool for acknowledging your worth.

2. **Set Boundaries**: When you recognize your significance, you set boundaries that protect your time, energy, and well-being. You don't let others take advantage of your kindness or overextend yourself for the sake of others. Healthy boundaries honor your worth and keep you grounded.

3. **Affirm Your Value**: Practice affirming your worth each day. This could be through affirmations, journaling, or simply taking a moment to reflect on the unique qualities that make you who you are. Remind yourself that you are worthy of love, respect, and success, just as you are.

4. **Stop Comparing**: One of the quickest ways to forget your significance is to compare yourself to others. Instead of measuring your worth against others' achievements or appearances, focus on your own unique journey. Embrace your individuality and celebrate the progress you're making.

5. **Live with Integrity**: When you understand your worth, you act with integrity. You make decisions that align with your values and principles, not based on what others expect or what's popular. Living with integrity reinforces your sense of significance.

6. **Serve Others**: One of the most powerful ways to acknowledge your significance is to serve others. By using your talents, time, and resources to help others, you reinforce your own value and contribute to the greater good of your community.

The Ripple Effect of Recognizing Your Worth

When you begin to understand and embrace your significance, the impact extends far beyond yourself. Recognizing your worth has a ripple effect on those around you.

As you honor yourself, you empower others to do the same. Your confidence and self-respect inspire others to recognize their own value, creating a culture of honor, respect, and mutual growth.

Understanding your worth also influences how you interact with the world. When you understand your significance, you make choices that align with your true purpose. You contribute to the world in a way that is meaningful and fulfilling, and in doing so, you inspire others to do the same. Your life becomes an example of living with honor and integrity, and this example can positively impact those around you.

Conclusion: Your Worth is Inherent

Understanding your significance is an essential part of living a life of honor. It requires you to recognize that your worth is inherent, not dependent on external achievements or others' perceptions.

When you fully embrace your value, you unlock the power to make decisions that align with your true self, build meaningful relationships, and contribute positively to the world around you.

In the next chapter, we will explore **Identity**—how knowing who you truly are allows you to act with clarity and confidence. Your journey of significance is just the beginning.

As you continue to explore these building blocks of honor, you will discover the strength that lies in knowing your worth and embracing your full potential.

You are significant. Your worth is inherent, and by embracing it, you honor yourself and the world around you.

Exercises:

- Write a list of qualities or achievements that make you proud of yourself.

Chapter 6: Identity – Embracing Who You Are

In a world that often pushes us to conform or live up to certain standards, one of the most powerful acts we can make is the decision to embrace who we are. Our identity isn't something that can be shaped by the expectations of others or dictated by the opinions around us. It's a deep understanding of ourselves, one that is rooted in our values, beliefs, experiences, and purpose. When we embrace who we are, we create a foundation of confidence, clarity, and integrity that empowers us to navigate life's challenges.

In this chapter, we will explore how embracing your identity is essential to living a life of honor and purpose. Understanding and accepting who you are allows you to make decisions that are true to yourself, foster authentic connections with others, and ultimately live with more meaning.

Embracing your identity isn't just about being comfortable with who you are; it's about honoring your unique story, your strengths, and your imperfections as part of the journey that makes you whole.

The Power of Self-Awareness

At the core of embracing who you are is self-awareness—the ability to understand your thoughts, feelings, actions, and desires. Self-awareness allows you to identify what truly matters to you and guides you in making decisions that are aligned with your authentic self.

Without self-awareness, it's easy to get caught up in the noise of external expectations or to lose sight of our values and purpose.

Self-awareness is more than just reflection; it's an ongoing practice of checking in with yourself, being honest about your strengths and weaknesses, and staying connected to your core. It's about recognizing the unique gifts and talents that make you who you are, while also acknowledging the areas where you still have room to grow.

This understanding of SELF as PRESENCE OF EXISTENCE forms the bedrock of your identity, and it informs every aspect of your life.

The more aware you are of who you truly are, the easier it becomes to live authentically. You no longer need to seek validation from others because you understand and appreciate your own worth.

You begin to trust your instincts, stand by your values, and make choices that reflect your true self. It's in this space of self-awareness that your identity becomes clearer, and your journey of self-discovery deepens.

The Role of Self-Acceptance

One of the most significant challenges in embracing your identity is learning to accept yourself fully. Self-acceptance is not about achieving perfection or being free from mistakes. It's about acknowledging that who you are—flaws, imperfections, and all—is enough.

When we embrace our true selves, we allow room for growth and change without feeling shame or guilt for not being perfect.

Self-acceptance frees you from the burden of trying to meet others' expectations or live up to an image of who you think you "should" be. Instead of focusing on what you lack, self-acceptance encourages you to celebrate your strengths, talents, and experiences. It allows you to see yourself as worthy of love, respect, and happiness, just as you are.

This act of acceptance can be difficult, especially in a culture that often values external appearances or superficial success. But the truth is, embracing who you are—every part of you—allows you to step into your fullest potential. You start living from a place of inner strength, knowing that your identity is not dependent on meeting certain standards or fitting into predefined boxes. Your value comes from simply being you.

Challenging External Expectations

From an early age, we are taught to conform to the expectations of others—whether it's parents, teachers, society, or peers. These external pressures shape how we see ourselves and can sometimes lead us to lose sight of who we truly are.

We may start living to meet other people's standards rather than following our own internal compass.

But part of embracing your identity is recognizing when you're being influenced by external forces and choosing to challenge those expectations.

It's about reclaiming your power to define yourself, regardless of what others think or say. You might feel pressure to follow certain career paths, look a certain way, or behave in specific ways to fit in. But honor comes from understanding that your identity is yours to define. To understand this fully is to embrace that to do an About-Face on Honor is to have a new meaning for the word honor and that is that the word honor serves as a mechanism that sorts one's priorities and sets them to values and the thought of a mission.

In this way (manner) breaking free from societal expectations doesn't mean rejecting the influence of others altogether. It simply means choosing to stay true to your own values and vision for your life. When you are in a group of people or in a family setting and values are shared and instilled and said to be importantly and your are taught them, then those are also values you choose to stay true to.

It's about finding the courage to trust yourself, even when others may not understand or approve. When you embrace who you are and live authentically, you empower yourself to create a life that is uniquely yours.

The Role of Purpose in Shaping Identity

One of the key elements of embracing your identity is understanding your purpose.

Purpose is the deeper why behind your actions and decisions. It is what gives your life direction, and when that purpose or functionality has actions towards kindness, joy and love, then purpose leads into meaning, and fulfillment.

Without a clear sense of purpose, it's easy to get lost in the chaos of everyday life or feel uncertain about your place in the world.

When you embrace your identity, you start to connect with your purpose on a deeper level. You begin to understand what drives you—whether it's helping others, pursuing creative passions, making a difference in your community, or building meaningful relationships.

No longer does HAVING MORE become a priority but instead BEING MORE for yourself, your family, friends, community, teammates and those you endear.

Your purpose becomes the compass that guides you as you navigate life, making choices that align with who you truly are.

Purpose and identity are intricately linked. When you know your purpose, you begin to live with intention. Every action you take, every relationship you nurture, and every decision you make is guided by your sense of self and your understanding of your place in the world.

The more clearly you define your purpose, the more clearly your identity becomes. Embracing your identity means recognizing that your purpose is a vital part of who you are.

The Importance of Defining Your Own Standards

As you embrace your identity, it becomes crucial to define your own standards—how you choose to live, what you value, and what you want to achieve. Your standards are the benchmarks by which you measure your actions and choices. They reflect the things that matter most to you, and they are grounded in your identity and purpose.

By setting your own standards, you free yourself from the pressure of living up to others' expectations. Instead of measuring your worth by someone else's definition of success, you create your own path based on what truly matters to you. You begin to live a life that reflects your values, rather than trying to meet external standards that don't align with your true self. It is when that path is known as the word manner, that the fashion and form of those manners seen as your actions show how you are representing your values.

Setting your own standards allows you to live with that integrity. You are no longer swayed by the opinions of others or the shifting trends of the world. You stay grounded in your own values and make choices that reflect your deepest truths. Your standards become the foundation of your identity.

Exercises:

- Create a visual representation (drawing, collage, or journal entry) of your identity, highlighting what makes you unique.

Chapter 7: Choices – Empowering Yourself Through Decisions

One of the most powerful aspects of being human is our ability to make choices. Every day, we are faced with decisions—big and small—that shape the trajectory of our lives.

The choices we make define who we are, what we value, and where we want to go. But with this power comes great responsibility. The decisions we make not only impact our own lives, but they ripple out to affect those around us.

In this chapter, we will explore the incredible power that comes with making conscious, intentional choices. We will uncover how the act of choosing can empower us to live with integrity, align with our deepest values, and create the life we desire.

Understanding the weight of our decisions and the ways in which they influence our reality is crucial to building a life of honor, purpose, and fulfillment. Let's dive deeper into the art of making choices that empower us to live authentically.

The Power of Choice

Choice is one of the greatest gifts we are given. It is a powerful tool for shaping our destiny.

However, many of us feel disconnected from this power. We might feel as though our circumstances or other people's expectations dictate our decisions. But in truth, the ability to choose is within us at every moment. From deciding how we react to challenges, to the way we navigate relationships, our choices are what define us.

It's easy to feel like life happens to us, that we are victims of our circumstances or the forces beyond our control. But the truth is, we always have a choice in how we respond.

Every decision, whether large or small, carries the potential to shape our experience. The power to choose is a cornerstone of personal empowerment. It allows us to break free from the confines of external expectations and live with intention.

When we realize that we have the ability to make choices, it unlocks a sense of personal agency.

This realization doesn't just make us more self-aware; it allows us to start actively crafting the life we want to live. We stop feeling like passive participants in our own story, and instead, we begin to feel like the authors of our own lives.

The Responsibility of Choice

While choices are empowering, they also come with responsibility. Every decision we make has consequences—whether immediate or long-term—that affect our lives and the lives of others. This responsibility is what makes our choices meaningful.

The consequences of our actions can be both positive and negative, and it's important to understand that we are accountable for the paths we choose to take.

As we grow older and gain more independence, we are often faced with decisions that carry significant weight—decisions about our careers, relationships, and personal goals.

It's essential to recognize that the choices we make in these areas set the tone for our future. And while we can't always control the outcomes of our decisions, we can choose how we approach them and how we respond to the results.

Being responsible for our choices means owning them—acknowledging the impact they have on ourselves and others. It's easy to blame others or circumstances when things don't turn out the way we hope, but true empowerment comes from recognizing that our choices are our own.

By taking full responsibility, we can learn from our decisions, course-correct if needed, and continue to move forward with purpose.

Intentional Decision-Making

One of the most important aspects of making empowered choices is the ability to make decisions intentionally. In a world filled with distractions and external pressures, it's easy to make decisions without considering their long-term impact.

We might make choices based on convenience, emotions, or the influence of others, rather than taking the time to reflect on what we truly want and what aligns with our values.

Intentional decision-making is about pausing to reflect on what matters most before making a choice. It's about considering how each decision fits within the larger context of your life and whether it aligns with your purpose, values, and goals.

Intentional decisions are made with clarity and foresight. They are grounded in a deep understanding of who you are and what you want to achieve. Decisions come also to prevent our own acceptance of undesired circumstances.

To make intentional decisions, start by cultivating self-awareness and mindfulness. Before reacting to a situation or rushing into a decision, take a moment to pause and evaluate. Ask yourself: *What do I truly want? How does this decision align with my values? What are the potential consequences of this choice?*

This intentional approach to decision-making ensures that your choices are not just reactive but proactive—each decision is a deliberate step toward the life you want to create.

Aligning Choices with Values

Our values are the guiding principles that shape our decisions. When we live in alignment with our values, our choices become more purposeful, and we experience a greater sense of fulfillment.

Honor, integrity, love, kindness, and respect—these are just a few of the values that might drive our decisions. When we understand our values and use them as a compass, it becomes much easier to make choices that reflect who we are at our core.

In contrast, when we make choices that are not aligned with our values, we experience dissonance and dissatisfaction. This is because our actions are out of sync with our authentic selves. Over time, this misalignment can erode our sense of self-worth and integrity, leading to feelings of regret, frustration, and confusion.

To live a life of honor, we must be intentional about aligning our choices with our values. Before making decisions, take time to reflect on your values and ask yourself: *Is this choice in alignment with what I stand for? Does this decision reflect the kind of person I want to be?* When we make choices that honor our values, we create a life that is authentic, fulfilling, and true to who we are.

Overcoming Fear in Decision-Making

Fear is one of the biggest barriers to making empowered decisions. Fear of failure, fear of judgment, or fear of the unknown can paralyze us, making it difficult to take action. It's natural to feel uncertain when faced with important decisions, but it's essential to recognize that fear is often a sign that we are stepping outside of our comfort zone and growing.

To overcome fear in decision-making, we must first acknowledge it without letting it control us. Fear doesn't have to hold us back. Instead of avoiding difficult decisions, we can learn to face them with courage and clarity. One way to do this is by reframing fear as an opportunity for growth. Every decision, even the difficult ones, offers a chance to learn, evolve, and become a stronger, more resilient person.

Practice shifting your mindset from fear to curiosity. Ask yourself: *What can I learn from this decision? How will this choice help me grow, even if it doesn't turn out the way I expect?* By viewing decisions through the lens of growth, we can make empowered choices, even in the face of uncertainty.

The Ripple Effect of Your Choices

Every decision we make has a ripple effect, influencing not only our lives but also the lives of those around us. This is why it's so important to be mindful of our choices.

What we do affects our relationships, our communities, and our world. When we choose to act with integrity, kindness, and honor, we inspire others to do the same. Conversely, when we make choices that are selfish or inconsiderate, we can contribute to division, resentment, and harm.

By making intentional, value-driven decisions, we create a positive ripple effect that extends beyond ourselves. Our choices have the potential to uplift, inspire, and empower those around us.

Every act of kindness, every decision made with integrity, every moment of respect contributes to a larger collective energy that fosters connection and growth. The very difference between purpose and meaning in life is in how we direct kindness, joy and love by our actions towards our SELF (inward) and to ares others.

Conclusion

In this chapter, we've explored how choices empower us to shape our lives and our futures. The decisions we make are the building blocks of our identity, values, purpose to which, by our actions, we direct toward meaningful decisions.

When we make choices that align with our authentic selves, we create a life that is meaningful, purposeful, and fulfilling. And as we make decisions intentionally, with responsibility and clarity, we empower not only ourselves but also the world around us.

As you move forward, remember that your choices are yours to make. Embrace the power of decision-making, align your choices with your values, and trust that every decision you make is a step toward living a life of honor, integrity, and purpose.

- **Exercises:**

- Reflect on a recent decision you made. What were the consequences, and what would you change, if anything?

Chapter 8: Attention – The Power of Focus

In a world flooded with distractions, the ability to focus has become one of the most valuable skills we can cultivate.

We live in an era where our attention is constantly being pulled in multiple directions. From social media notifications to the never-ending stream of information, it's easy to feel scattered, overwhelmed, and disconnected. Yet, the true power of focus lies in its ability to bring clarity, productivity, and meaning to our lives.

By learning how to harness the power of attention, we can reclaim control over where we invest our time, energy, and mental resources, ultimately leading us to greater fulfillment and success.

In this chapter, we will explore how attention—the act of focusing on what truly matters—can empower us to live with intention, achieve our goals, and deepen our relationships.

We will dive into the science of attention, how distractions impact our lives, and most importantly, how to train our minds to focus on what is truly important.

By the end of this chapter, you will have a deeper understanding of the power of focus and practical tools to enhance your attention in a world that often seems to pull you in a thousand different directions.

The Power of Focus

Focus is more than just a mental skill—it's a superpower. When we focus our attention on something, we channel our energy into it, giving it the power to grow and thrive.

Whether it's a personal goal, a relationship, or a creative endeavor, the act of focusing allows us to direct our energy and resources in a way that creates momentum and progress.

Without focus, we risk being pulled in so many directions that we never make meaningful progress on anything. Think of focus as the lens of a camera—it brings clarity to a blurry world. When our attention is scattered, everything appears fuzzy and overwhelming. But when we focus, we narrow our attention to what truly matters, and we begin to see clearly.

Focus is also essential for learning and growth. To acquire new skills or deepen our understanding of a subject, we must direct our attention and energy toward that subject. Without sustained focus, learning becomes fragmented, and progress slows down.

However, when we commit to focusing our attention on a specific task or goal, we accelerate our growth and move closer to our desired outcomes.

The Challenge of Distractions

In today's fast-paced world, distractions are everywhere. From the constant barrage of notifications on our phones to the pressures of social media and work, our attention is constantly being hijacked.

These distractions are not only a source of stress—they can also undermine our ability to live with purpose and intentionality.

The problem with distractions is that they don't just take our attention away from what matters—they often replace it with something that is not meaningful or fulfilling. Instead of focusing on our goals or our relationships, we might find ourselves mindlessly scrolling through social media, watching endless videos, or checking our email for the hundredth time in a day.

Over time, these distractions take a toll on our ability to concentrate and maintain sustained attention. When our attention is constantly divided, it becomes difficult to engage deeply with anything, leaving us feeling unproductive, restless, and disconnected.

But the good news is that focus is a skill we can improve. By recognizing the impact of distractions and making conscious decisions to limit them, we can train ourselves to be more present and focused on what truly matters.

The Science of Attention

Attention is not a fixed trait—it's a cognitive skill that we can develop and refine over time. Research in neuroscience has shown that our brains are capable of focusing on a specific task for extended periods, but only when we consciously train them to do so.

The more we practice focused attention, the stronger our attention span becomes, just like any other muscle in our body.

There are different types of attention: selective attention, sustained attention, and divided attention. Selective attention is the ability to focus on a specific task or object while filtering out distractions.

Sustained attention refers to the ability to concentrate on a task for an extended period. Divided attention, on the other hand, is when we attempt to multitask—something our brains are not naturally good at.

The key to mastering focus is to improve our selective and sustained attention while minimizing divided attention. This means eliminating distractions and creating an environment that allows us to concentrate deeply on the task at hand.

The more we practice focusing on one thing at a time, the stronger our ability to maintain attention becomes, leading to greater efficiency and clarity.

Training Your Attention

Focus is a skill, and like any skill, it requires practice. Here are several strategies you can use to improve your attention and train your mind to focus:

1. **Create a Focused Environment**: One of the easiest ways to improve focus is to eliminate distractions. This might mean turning off notifications, creating a quiet space to work, or organizing your environment so that it supports concentration.

2. **Practice Mindfulness**: Mindfulness is the practice of being fully present in the moment. When we practice mindfulness, we train our minds to focus on the here and now, without getting lost in distractions or worries. You can practice mindfulness through meditation, deep breathing, or simply paying attention to your surroundings and sensations.

3. **Use the Pomodoro Technique**: This technique involves working in short bursts of focused time, typically 25 minutes, followed by a 5-minute break. After four rounds, take a longer break. This method helps train your brain to focus in short, manageable intervals, preventing burnout and maintaining high levels of productivity.

4. **Limit Multitasking**: Multitasking may seem like an efficient way to get things done, but research shows that it actually decreases productivity and increases stress. Instead of trying to do many things at once, focus on one task at a time. By giving each task your full attention, you will complete it more effectively and efficiently.

5. **Prioritize Your Tasks**: Focus is not just about concentration—it's also about prioritization. Identify the tasks that are most important and focus on them first. This ensures that your attention is directed toward what matters most, rather than getting caught up in less important tasks that don't align with your goals.

6. **Take Regular Breaks**: Our brains can only maintain intense focus for so long. To avoid mental fatigue and maintain productivity, it's important to take regular breaks. Use these breaks to recharge, stretch, or take a walk. This will help your mind stay fresh and focused throughout the day.

Focus and Personal Growth

Focus is an essential ingredient for personal growth. When we focus on our goals and dedicate time and energy to achieving them, we create momentum that propels us forward.

Whether we are working toward a career aspiration, improving a skill, or deepening our relationships, sustained focus is what enables us to make consistent progress.

Focus also plays a critical role in our mental and emotional well-being.

When we are able to focus on the present moment, we reduce feelings of anxiety, stress, and overwhelm.

By focusing on what we can control and letting go of what is beyond our reach, we can cultivate a sense of peace and clarity.

Additionally, when we focus on developing ourselves—whether through self-reflection, learning, or growth—we move closer to our highest potential. Focus allows us to identify what truly matters in our lives, and it gives us the energy and determination to pursue it relentlessly.

The Role of Attention in Relationships

Our ability to focus also plays a vital role in our relationships. In a world where distractions are constant, giving someone our undivided attention is a powerful act of respect and care.

When we are truly present with others—whether in conversation, shared activities, or simply spending time together—we build deeper connections and foster trust.

Listening attentively, making eye contact, and being fully engaged in the moment are all ways to show others that we value them. This level of focus strengthens relationships and helps to cultivate mutual respect, understanding, and empathy.

Conclusion

In this chapter, we've explored the transformative power of focus and attention. Focus is a skill that can be developed and refined, and it is one of the most important tools we have for living a life of purpose and intention. By recognizing the distractions that pull us away from what matters and committing to practices that enhance our attention, we can create a life of clarity, productivity, and fulfillment.

As you move forward, ask yourself: *Where is my attention going? Am I focusing on what truly matters? How can I cultivate greater focus in my life?* The power to shape your life is in your hands—and it begins with where you choose to direct your attention.

Exercises:

- Practice focusing on one task without distractions for 10 minutes. Journal your thoughts on the experience.

Chapter 9: Building Meaningful Relationships

At the heart of a fulfilling life lies connection—connection to others, to the world, and to ourselves. It is through our relationships that we experience love, support, challenge, and growth.

Whether with family, friends, romantic partners, or colleagues, relationships shape our emotional landscape and play a vital role in our overall well-being. Yet, in today's fast-paced, often fragmented world, building and maintaining meaningful relationships can seem like a challenging task.

In this chapter, we'll explore the principles and practices of cultivating deep, authentic connections that nourish and enrich our lives.

We'll focus on how to create relationships built on trust, respect, and mutual understanding. We'll also examine how our personal growth, communication skills, and ability to show up for others can strengthen the bonds we form.

Relationships are not simply about the people we know but the way we engage with them—how we show up, the energy we give, and the love and care we share. By the end of this chapter, you will gain a deeper understanding of how to foster relationships that bring joy, growth, and meaning to your life.

The Importance of Meaningful Relationships

In our increasingly individualistic society, it's easy to overlook the fundamental need for deep, authentic relationships.

Modern life often emphasizes independence, achievement, and personal success, leading many to focus more on career advancement or material accomplishments than on building real connections.

However, research consistently shows that meaningful relationships are essential for happiness and emotional health.

Relationships provide us with the support and companionship that help us navigate life's challenges. Whether it's the bond with a close friend who listens without judgment, the encouragement of a family member who believes in us, or the love of a partner who shares our dreams, these connections remind us that we are not alone. They give us a sense of belonging, security, and purpose.

Moreover, meaningful relationships help us grow. Through our interactions with others, we learn more about ourselves, our values, and our capacity for empathy, patience, and love.

Relationships challenge us to become better versions of ourselves, prompting us to reflect on our behaviors, actions, and attitudes. When we invest in meaningful relationships, we build a support system that fosters both our personal and collective growth.

The Foundations of Strong Relationships

Building meaningful relationships is not a passive process—it requires effort, intention, and care. There are several key foundations that support the growth of these relationships:

1. **Trust**: Trust is the cornerstone of any strong relationship. It is built through consistency, reliability, and openness. Trust allows us to be vulnerable with others, knowing that they will honor our feelings and boundaries. Without trust, relationships become shallow and strained.

To build trust, we must demonstrate integrity and be honest in our actions and words.

2. **Respect**: Respect is a mutual understanding that each person's thoughts, feelings, and experiences are valid. When we respect others, we honor their autonomy, ideas, and choices. Respectful relationships are rooted in equality, where both parties feel heard and valued. It's essential to understand that respect is not a given—it must be cultivated through active listening, empathy, and non-judgmental acceptance.

3. **Vulnerability**: True connection requires vulnerability—the willingness to share our authentic selves, flaws and all. In a world that often encourages perfection, it's easy to hide behind masks of strength and confidence. However, meaningful relationships thrive when we allow ourselves to be vulnerable. This means showing our true emotions, admitting our mistakes, and being open about our struggles. Vulnerability fosters intimacy and creates a space for others to do the same, deepening the connection.

4. **Communication**: Effective communication is the lifeblood of any relationship. It involves not just speaking clearly but also listening deeply. Communication is an ongoing process of expressing needs, clarifying misunderstandings, and making sure both parties feel heard and understood. Poor communication can lead to conflict and misunderstandings, whereas clear and compassionate communication strengthens bonds.

5. **Shared Values**: While differences in opinion or background are inevitable, relationships are often strongest when both individuals share common values. Whether it's a shared sense of purpose, similar life goals, or aligned ethical principles, these commonalities create a strong foundation for understanding and collaboration. When you and another person are on the same page regarding the big picture, it fosters a sense of unity and shared direction.

The Role of Boundaries

While trust, respect, and vulnerability are crucial to meaningful relationships, maintaining healthy boundaries is just as important.

Boundaries help define where one person ends and another begins, creating space for each individual to honor their own needs and well-being within the relationship.

Boundaries can be emotional, physical, or even digital. For instance, emotional boundaries help us manage the intensity of our feelings, preventing one person from becoming overly responsible for another's emotional state.

Physical boundaries might involve setting limits on how much physical closeness we're comfortable with. Digital boundaries could mean deciding when and how we communicate online.

Healthy relationships respect each person's boundaries, and these boundaries help preserve individual identities. Without boundaries, relationships can become codependent, stifling, or draining.

Setting clear and respectful boundaries ensures that both individuals can grow independently while nurturing their connection with one another.

Navigating Conflict in Relationships

Conflict is a natural part of any relationship, but how we navigate conflict can either strengthen or weaken our bonds. Conflict arises from differences in perspective, needs, or values—and it's inevitable in relationships.

However, when handled with care, conflict can be an opportunity for growth, deeper understanding, and improved communication.

Here are some strategies for navigating conflict in a healthy way:

1. **Stay Calm and Centered**: In moments of disagreement, it's easy to become defensive or reactive. However, staying calm and taking a step back can help you approach the situation with more clarity and patience. Take a deep breath, and allow yourself a moment to reflect before responding.

2. **Listen Actively**: Conflict often arises from miscommunication or misunderstandings. Listening actively to the other person's perspective helps to clarify their feelings and needs. Show empathy by acknowledging their emotions and validating their point of view, even if you don't fully agree.

3. **Focus on the Issue, Not the Person**: When conflict arises, it's important to focus on the issue at hand, not on attacking the other person. Avoid blame and name-calling, as these behaviors only escalate tensions. Instead, use "I" statements to express how you feel, such as "I feel frustrated when…" or "I need…"

4. **Seek Resolution, Not Victory**: In healthy relationships, the goal is not to "win" an argument but to find a solution that works for both parties. This may involve compromise, forgiveness, or finding creative ways to meet each other's needs. Keep the focus on resolving the issue constructively, rather than on "being right."

5. **Learn from Conflict**: Each conflict presents an opportunity for growth. After a disagreement, take time to reflect on what you learned about yourself, the other person, and the relationship. Did you uncover a hidden need? Did you discover a new way to communicate more effectively? Embrace conflict as an opportunity for improvement.

Building Relationships with Yourself

While much of this chapter focuses on building meaningful relationships with others, it's important to remember that the foundation of all relationships starts with how we relate to ourselves. Our relationship with ourselves—our self-respect, self-compassion, and self-awareness—shapes how we engage with others.

When we cultivate a positive relationship with ourselves, we bring our best selves to our interactions. Self-love, self-care, and self-acceptance create the inner security necessary to build authentic relationships with others.

If we struggle with self-worth or self-doubt, it can be challenging to form healthy connections, as we may unconsciously seek validation or approval from others. Building a strong relationship with yourself allows you to approach relationships from a place of confidence and openness.

Conclusion: The Power of Connection

In this chapter, we've explored how to build meaningful relationships— those that are built on trust, respect, vulnerability, communication, and shared values.

Meaningful relationships are essential to our well-being, personal growth, and happiness. By investing in these connections and learning to navigate conflict and set healthy boundaries, we can create relationships that nourish our lives.

Remember, relationships are not static; they require continuous effort, care, and attention. Whether it's strengthening bonds with family, deepening friendships, or building romantic partnerships, the quality of your relationships is one of the most significant factors in shaping your happiness and fulfillment.

As you move forward, ask yourself: *What type of relationships do I want to cultivate?How can I show up for the people I care about in a more meaningful way?* By answering these questions, you can begin to create relationships that bring value, joy, and purpose into your life—and ultimately, into the lives of those around you.

Exercises:

- Have a conversation with a close friend or family member using the principles of honor you've learned.

Chapter 10: Navigating Hard Times with Honor

Life is full of uncertainties. We all encounter challenges, setbacks, and moments of hardship that test our strength and resilience.

Whether facing personal loss, career struggles, health issues, or societal pressures, these difficult times often leave us feeling lost, uncertain, and vulnerable. But in the midst of adversity, there is an opportunity to stay grounded, find purpose, and rise with integrity.

The key to enduring hardship lies in how we navigate it—and this is where honor becomes our guiding light.

Honor, as we've explored in the previous chapters, is more than just a concept; it's a powerful force that can shape our actions, decisions, and relationships. In this chapter, we will focus on how honor can guide us through hard times—helping us maintain our values, our sense of self, and our dignity when everything around us feels uncertain.

The Role of Honor in Difficult Times

In times of struggle, it's easy to feel disoriented and unsure of how to proceed. Our emotions might cloud our judgment, and the pressure of external circumstances can tempt us to compromise our integrity.

Yet, honor has the potential to act as an anchor in the storm. It is the foundation that allows us to stay true to ourselves, even when everything seems to be falling apart.

Honor in difficult times isn't about denying the pain or pretending everything is fine. Rather, it is about how we face adversity and the choices we make in the process. It challenges us to respond to hardship with dignity, compassion, and respect—both for ourselves and others.

When we act honorably, we make decisions that reflect our true values, even in the face of overwhelming circumstances.

Cultivating Resilience Through Honor

One of the most important aspects of navigating hard times is resilience— the ability to bounce back after setbacks and continue moving forward despite obstacles.

Resilience doesn't mean that we don't feel pain or that we always have to be strong. It means that we have the ability to face difficulty with grace, learn from our experiences, and adapt to new realities.

Honor is closely tied to resilience. When we face challenges, honor gives us the courage to keep going. It reminds us that our worth is not defined by our circumstances and that we have the strength to endure hardship with integrity. By staying true to our principles, we can find the inner strength to persevere, even when the road ahead is unclear.

In moments of hardship, it's easy to fall into the trap of self-pity or resentment. However, honor invites us to rise above these negative emotions. It challenges us to see adversity not as a roadblock but as an opportunity for growth.

The trials we face can shape us into stronger, wiser individuals if we face them with the right mindset and principles. Honor, in this sense, becomes a powerful tool for building resilience.

The Power of Perspective

When navigating hard times, one of the most important skills is the ability to shift our perspective.

Challenges often bring with them feelings of helplessness or frustration, but it is how we perceive these challenges that ultimately defines our experience.

Honor helps us cultivate a mindset that sees adversity as part of life's journey—something to be faced, not feared.

Honor reminds us that when we act on our fears —because of what we value—and that action avoids consequences, we have come to know fear as a self-protection mechanism used to make a decision to act on behalf of ourselves or others. In this way (manner) acting on a fear that triggered us to take action is observable SELF-LOVE.

When we step out of the way of a car coming towards us in order not to be hit, we used fear as a SELF-protection mechanism that triggered others seeing that stepping out of the way of the car as our form of observable SELF-love.

In these difficult situations, honor helps us focus on what we can control, rather than what we cannot. It encourages us to take responsibility for our actions, choices, and responses.

By shifting our perspective from victimhood to empowerment, we recognize that we have the ability to respond to hardship in ways that align with our values.

For example, a personal loss may make us feel devastated and powerless. However, through the lens of honor, we might shift our focus to the lessons we've learned, the strength we've discovered within ourselves, and the ways in which we can continue to honor the memory of what we've lost. In this same manner, the feeling of loss we have can be said to be rooted in first there being an appreciation for what once was that no longer is. The feeling of loss stems from appreciation.

In doing so, we reclaim our power and create meaning in the face of grief.

Living with Integrity During Challenging Times

One of the most challenging aspects of hard times is the temptation to abandon our values in the name of survival or convenience.

In the heat of the moment, it can be easy to rationalize actions that go against our principles, especially when we feel cornered or desperate.

Yet, maintaining our integrity during challenging times is one of the most powerful ways to honor ourselves.

Living with integrity means making choices that reflect who we are, even when it's difficult. It means refusing to compromise on what we believe is right, even when the world around us is urging us to do otherwise. The true GRIT of integrity acts as cement between all the building blocks of honor to comprise to form your authentic CHARACTER.

This manner of integrity ensures that, no matter the challenges we face, we can look ourselves in the mirror and feel proud of the way we've navigated the storm.

This can be particularly difficult in the face of financial strain, personal loss, or professional setbacks, where the temptation to cut corners or abandon one's values might seem like the quickest way out.

However, honor encourages us to consider the long-term consequences of our choices. Choosing integrity, even when it's hard, is ultimately what helps us build a life of meaning, purpose, and self-respect.

The Importance of Self-Compassion

In the face of difficulty, we are often our own harshest critics. We might blame ourselves for the situation we're in, feel ashamed of our perceived weaknesses, or judge ourselves for not being able to "handle" the challenge better.

Honor, however, invites us to practice self-compassion—to treat ourselves with the same kindness, understanding, and respect that we would offer a close friend. In these acts we find the utmost meaning of kindness, joy and love in one another. In these ways (manners) we find a new meaning for the word inspiration. As such, INSPIRATION IS AN INVITATION TOWARDS UTMOST MEANING.

This self-compassion and compassion towards others is not about making excuses or avoiding responsibility. Rather, it is about recognizing that we, like everyone else, are human.

We make mistakes, we face hardships, and we experience setbacks. Through honor, we learn to embrace these moments as part of our growth, rather than as failures.

When we practice self-compassion, we give ourselves the space to feel our emotions—whether that's sadness, frustration, or fear—without judgment.

We allow ourselves to process and heal, rather than suppress or ignore our feelings.

This self-awareness and acceptance create the mental and emotional strength, an utmost meaning needed to continue moving forward with honor and dignity.

The Role of Support Systems

No one navigates hard times alone, and it is in our relationships that we find some of our greatest sources of strength. Support systems—whether through family, friends, mentors, or counselors—provide us with guidance, understanding, and encouragement during times of struggle.

Honor not only involves showing up for ourselves but also showing up for others. In difficult times, it is essential to both seek support when we need it and offer support when others are in need.

By maintaining our commitment to honor in our relationships, we strengthen the bonds that allow us to endure hard times together.

In your own journey, ask yourself: *Who can I turn to for support? How can I be a source of strength for others?*

By leaning into the support of those we trust and offering the same to those who need it, we create a network of compassion and resilience that helps us weather any storm.

Moving Forward with Purpose and Directing it towards Kindness, Joy and Love

Navigating hard times is never easy, and no one is immune to life's challenges. However, through the lens of honor, we can approach adversity with courage, resilience, and integrity.

Rather than seeing hardship as a punishment, honor allows us to view it as an INSPIRATION towards opportunities for growth, learning, and personal transformation.

The trials we face shape us into the individuals we are meant to be, and honor provides us with the tools to navigate these trials with dignity and self-respect.

Whether it's in moments of grief, disappointment, or failure, we can choose to meet life's challenges with strength, grace, and a deep commitment to our values.

In this chapter, we've explored how honor can guide us through difficult times—helping us maintain our integrity, resilience, and perspective.

As you face your own challenges, remember that the path forward may not always be easy, but through honor, you have the power to navigate the storm and emerge stronger on the other side. Remember that with honor, the meaning of the word path is the word manner, and it is with your manners you reflect honor onto others by your actions.

So, as you move through life's inevitable struggles, ask yourself: *How can I approach this challenge with honor? How can I stay true to my values and integrity, even when it's hard?* By embracing honor in the face of adversity, you create the foundation for a life of resilience, purpose, and unshakable strength.

Exercises:

- Reflect on a difficult time in your life. How did you handle it? How could you have used the building blocks of honor to navigate it differently?

Chapter 11: Moving Forward: Living with Purpose and Integrity

As we come to the final chapter of this journey, it's time to reflect on everything we've learned, the principles we've explored, and how we can take them forward into the future.

Life is not a static experience; it's a continuous journey of growth, self-discovery, and transformation. With each chapter, we've built a foundation that empowers us to navigate the complexities of life with clarity and strength. But now, we must look ahead—moving forward with a sense of purpose and integrity.

Living with purpose and integrity isn't just about making wise choices when things are easy. It's about sustaining those values in the face of challenges, staying true to who we are when life becomes complicated, and moving forward with a vision that aligns with our deepest principles.

In this chapter, we'll explore how to apply the lessons of honor, resilience, and self-awareness to shape a life driven by meaning and integrity. We'll look at how to move forward in a way that reflects our true selves, guided by the knowledge that living with purpose is the key to living a fulfilled life.

The Power of Purpose

Purpose is the compass that directs our actions, fuels our decisions, and provides us with a sense of meaning.

Without purpose or functionality, life can feel aimless—like we're going through the motions without ever truly understanding the "why" behind what we do.

Purpose gives us clarity, motivation, and focus, helping us make decisions that reflect our core values. Aligning that purpose towards kindness, joy and love brings meaning to life.

In the context of this book, living with purpose means we are doing just that; by actively aligning our actions with our deepest beliefs and goals. It's about knowing who we are, understanding our values, and setting clear intentions for how we want to show up in the world. It is also about adding new meaning to the word BELIEF and measures of honor, BELIEF IS AN IMAGE OF ACHIEVEMENT.

This kind of intentional living requires self-reflection and an ongoing commitment to growth.

To live with purpose, we must ask ourselves: *What truly matters to me? What do I want to contribute to the world? How can my actions reflect the honor, integrity, and values I hold dear?*

Answering these questions allows us to move forward with intention, shaping a life that's not just about surviving but about thriving in alignment with our authentic selves.

Integrity as the Foundation

Integrity is the bedrock upon which purposeful living is built. Without integrity, our actions become disconnected from our values, and we risk falling into a pattern of self-deception or compromise. Integrity ensures that our inner beliefs align with our outward behavior, creating harmony between who we are on the inside and how we show up in the world. Without integrity the connectivity between your building blocks of honor (in you) to uprise to become your authentic CHARACTER does not happen.

Living with integrity means doing what's right, even when it's not easy. It means acting in ways that reflect our values and staying true to our principles, even in the face of temptation or pressure to act otherwise.

Integrity requires consistency and courage—it's about being the same person in every situation, regardless of external circumstances.

As you move forward, remember that integrity isn't just a one-time decision—it's a daily practice. It's in the small choices we make: how we treat others, how we honor our commitments, and how we live out our values when no one is watching. When we live with integrity, we create a life that's grounded in authenticity and trust.

The Intersection of Honor and Purpose

Honor, as we've explored in earlier chapters, is the recognition of one's own worth and the respect shown to others. It's not just about receiving recognition—it's about living in a way that reflects our deepest values, creating a positive impact on the world around us.

When we live with honor, we align our actions with our highest ideals. This means that our pursuit of purpose is not self-serving; instead, it becomes a service to something greater—whether that's our family, community, career, or the world at large. Purpose and honor are deeply intertwined: honor gives us the framework to live with integrity, and purpose gives us a reason to live out our honor.

Living with honor and purpose means understanding that our decisions are never isolated—that they give rise to utmost meaning and they ripple out and affect the world around us.

Every action we take has the potential to create positive change, whether we're aware of it or not. This realization empowers us to live with intention, knowing that our choices matter, and they have the power to shape the world for the better.

Overcoming Obstacles with Purpose and Integrity

While moving forward with purpose and integrity sounds ideal, it's not without its challenges. Life often throws obstacles our way—doubts, distractions, and setbacks that can derail us from our path. However, it's during these tough moments that our commitment to purpose and integrity becomes most crucial.

The ability to stay focused on our purpose, even in the face of adversity, is what sets those who succeed from those who falter. Integrity helps us stay grounded and committed to our path, even when external forces try to lead us astray.

When we encounter challenges, it's important to remember that setbacks are a natural part of the journey—not an indication that we should give up on our dreams.

In these moments, ask yourself: *How can I stay true to my values and move forward despite the difficulty? What does it mean to maintain my integrity and purpose, even in the face of challenges?* By consistently aligning your actions with your values, you build the resilience needed to navigate the inevitable struggles that arise along the way.

Reflection as a Tool for Growth

Living with purpose and integrity requires constant reflection. As we move forward, it's essential to periodically check in with ourselves to assess whether we're still aligned with our values and goals.

SELF-reflection helps us stay on track, make necessary adjustments, and continue growing in the direction we want to go.

Regular reflection allows us to acknowledge our progress, celebrate our wins, and learn from our mistakes. It helps us remain humble and open to growth, knowing that living with purpose is not a destination but a continuous journey of evolution. When we reflect, we give ourselves the space to recalibrate, ensuring that we're living authentically and with intention.

Living with Legacy in Mind

One of the most powerful ways to live with purpose and integrity is by considering the legacy we want to leave behind. We won't be around forever, but the impact we make today can influence generations to come.

By aligning our actions with our values, we can create a legacy that reflects the best of who we are.

Living with legacy in mind means acting in ways that not only benefit us but also benefit others. It's about using our talents, resources, and opportunities to create a better world—whether that's through our work, our relationships, or our contributions to society. A life lived with purpose and integrity leaves behind a positive impact that can inspire others to do the same.

Moving Forward: The Road Ahead

Now that we've explored how to live with purpose and integrity, the next step is action. It's time to take everything we've learned and put it into practice.

Living with purpose doesn't happen overnight—it requires daily commitment, intentional decisions, and the courage to stay true to ourselves.

Start by setting clear, meaningful goals that align with your values. Break them down into actionable steps and begin making progress, no matter how small. Hold yourself accountable, but also practice self-compassion when setbacks occur. Remember, this journey isn't about perfection—it's about consistency and growth.

As you move forward, continue to reflect on your purpose, your integrity, and the legacy you wish to create. Commit to living each day with honor, using every opportunity to align your actions with your deepest values. And, when life gets difficult, remember that your purpose and integrity will always guide you through.

In the end, living with purpose and integrity aligning that purpose towards kindness, joy and love to lead to utmost meaning is the key to a life well-lived. It's a life rooted in authenticity, guided by values, and focused on making a positive impact in the world.

By embracing this approach, you can confidently move forward into the future, knowing that every step you take is aligned with your true self.

As you embark on this next chapter of your life, carry these principles with you: purpose, integrity, honor, and growth. They will be your compass as you navigate the future—ensuring that you live not only for today but also for the legacy you will leave behind.

Conclusion: The Power of Honor in Action

As we reach the end of this journey, it's time to reflect on the powerful themes we've explored and consider how they come together in our everyday lives.

Honor, as we've seen, is not just a lofty ideal—it's a living, breathing principle that shapes our thoughts, actions, and relationships. It's a foundation upon which we can build a life of purpose, integrity, and meaning. But as we've also discovered, honor is not something we merely think about; it is something we actively practice and embody. It is through action that honor becomes a force that drives us toward greater fulfillment and impact.

Throughout this book, we've examined the building blocks that enable us to live with honor: recognizing our independent authenticity, having faith in ourselves and the process, being present in the moment, understanding our significance, embracing who we are, making empowered choices, focusing our attention, building meaningful relationships, and navigating hard times with resilience. Each of these chapters has contributed to a holistic understanding of how honor shapes every aspect of our lives. But in the end, it is how we put these concepts into practice that determines whether we truly live in alignment with honor.

Honor as a Living Practice

Honor is not a static concept; it requires continuous effort, attention, and intention. It's easy to talk about honor, to agree with its importance in theory, but the real challenge lies in living it out every day. Honor demands that we remain committed to our values, even when it's difficult, and that we consistently show up as our true selves, no matter the circumstances.

As we've learned, honor is about more than just our internal state; it extends outward into the world around us. It is reflected in how we treat others, how we make decisions, and how we confront challenges. When we live with honor, our actions speak louder than words.

Honor becomes evident not just in our thoughts or beliefs, but in the way we interact with the world—how we take responsibility for our actions, how we build meaningful connections, and how we navigate both the good and the bad times.

The Ripple Effect of Honor

One of the most powerful aspects of honor is its ripple effect. When we act with honor, we not only elevate ourselves but also influence the world around us.

Our actions can INSPIRE others to live with integrity, just as the actions of others inspire us. Honor is contagious. It encourages trust, builds respect, and fosters relationships that are rooted in mutual understanding and compassion.

Consider the many ways in which honor spreads: when we honor ourselves, we show others how to honor themselves. When we honor others, we create a space where they feel seen and respected. Honor also leads to greater collaboration, because it fosters an environment of trust, reliability, and shared values.

By acting with honor, we help to create a culture of honor in our communities, workplaces, and families, transforming not only our individual lives but also the collective experience.

Honor in the Face of Adversity

Honor is especially powerful when faced with adversity. Life isn't always easy, and we are bound to encounter difficult times.

It's in these moments that our commitment to honor is tested. Will we remain true to our values, even when the world seems to be falling apart? Will we hold onto our integrity, even when it seems like the easier path is to compromise?

Throughout this book, we've explored how honor can guide us during tough times—whether in navigating personal challenges, facing uncertainty, or dealing with conflict.

Honor provides us with a strong foundation, one that can anchor us when everything around us feels uncertain. By keeping our focus on what truly matters—our values, our purpose, our sense of integrity—we can rise above adversity and emerge stronger.

When we live with honor in the face of hardship, we show resilience. We demonstrate that we are not defined by external circumstances but by the strength of our character. And in doing so, we become beacons of hope and inspiration for others who may be struggling.

Our actions can serve as a reminder that even in the toughest of times, it's possible to live with dignity, respect, and purpose.

The Journey Ahead

As we conclude this exploration of honor, remember that the journey is far from over. In fact, it's just beginning.

Honor is not a one-time achievement but a lifelong commitment to living with purpose, integrity, and authenticity. Each day presents new opportunities to practice honor in all areas of our lives—whether in our relationships, our work, or our personal growth.

The key to living honorably is to stay present, stay true to ourselves, and stay committed to the values that guide us. Honor doesn't require perfection, but it does require consistency and a willingness to grow. It's about making decisions that align with who we are and who we want to become. And even when we fall short, we have the grace to rise again, learn from our mistakes, and keep moving forward.

Honor in Action: A Call to Live Your Best Life

Now, as you move forward, remember that honor is something you can put into action every day. It's in the small moments—how you treat others, how you show up for yourself, how you make choices that reflect your values. Every decision is an opportunity to embody the principles you've learned.

Honor is not just an abstract idea or a philosophical concept; it's something tangible. It's in how you speak to someone who is struggling, how you hold yourself accountable, how you make choices that reflect your best self.

Every act of honor is a step toward living a life that is meaningful, authentic, and aligned with your truest values.

Living with honor isn't always easy, but it's always worth it. The world needs people who are willing to live with integrity, who are willing to stand up for what is right, and who are willing to show others the power of respect, kindness, and self-awareness. You have the power to be one of those people.

So, take what you've learned in this book and use it as a foundation for your life. Practice honor in every aspect of your journey.

Be present, make choices that reflect your values, nurture your relationships, and hold fast to your integrity. As you move forward, honor will continue to guide you, giving you the strength to live with purpose, resilience, and authenticity.

In the end, the power of honor is the power to shape your life, your relationships, and your impact on the world. It's a power that starts within you but extends far beyond you, creating a legacy that can inspire others to do the same.

Live honorably. Live with purpose and integrity-led meaning in life. Live with integrity. And watch the world transform around you.

Exercises:

- Write a letter to your future self about the changes you've made and the path you want to continue on.

Additional Resources for Young Adult Readers (Ages 12-18)

Suggested Reading:

1. Books:

- *The 7 Habits of Highly Effective Teens* by Sean Covey – A teen-focused adaptation of the classic book, teaching the power of habits and mindset for personal success and growth.

- *Wonder* by R.J. Palacio – A heartfelt story about kindness, self-acceptance, and overcoming challenges, perfect for building empathy and understanding identity.

- *You Are a Badass* by Jen Sincero – A motivational guide designed to help teens believe in themselves and take control of their lives.

- *The Hate U Give* by Angie Thomas – A compelling novel exploring identity, social justice, and how to stand up for what's right.

- *The Four Agreements* by Don Miguel Ruiz – A practical guide for living a life of honor, clarity, and authenticity, written in a way that's relatable for young adults.

- *Big Magic* by Elizabeth Gilbert – A book about creativity, overcoming fear, and embracing your authentic self, helping teens to trust in their unique talents and abilities.

- *Untamed* by Glennon Doyle – A book about finding your voice and embracing your true identity, aimed at young people navigating change and personal growth.

2. Articles:

- *How to Build Your Self-Esteem in 5 Simple Steps* – Learn practical techniques to boost self-esteem, overcome insecurity, and honor your true self.

- *The Power of Vulnerability* – Understanding how embracing vulnerability can lead to stronger relationships and deeper self-awareness.

- *The Benefits of Mindfulness for Teens* – An article that highlights the importance of mindfulness for reducing stress, increasing focus, and improving emotional well-being.
- *Why Authenticity Matters: The Key to True Confidence* – Exploring the power of being true to yourself in a world full of pressures and expectations.

3. **Podcasts:**

   - *The Self-Helpless Podcast* – A fun, relatable podcast that dives into topics like self-improvement, mental health, and personal growth, with a focus on how to apply these lessons to everyday life.
   - *The Teen Life Coach Podcast* – Offers guidance for teens on self-discovery, overcoming challenges, and building resilience.
   - *Feel Better, Live More* by Dr. Rangan Chatterjee – A podcast that covers topics like mental health, mindfulness, and practical ways to feel your best.
   - *The Mindful Kind* – Short and accessible episodes on mindfulness and mental well-being, perfect for young adults seeking more peace and presence in their lives.

Support Networks for Young Adults:

Mentorship and Counseling:

- **Find a Mentor:**

  - Mentorship can be an invaluable resource for guidance and support during the teen years. Look for mentors through school programs, extracurricular activities, or community centers. Trusted adults such as teachers, coaches, or family friends can provide a safe space for advice and wisdom.
  - Platforms like **iCouldBe**, **MentorMe**, or local community organizations may also offer formal mentorship programs specifically designed for young people.

- **Therapists and Counselors:**
  - If you're facing challenges like anxiety, stress, or relationship issues, speaking with a therapist can help you develop coping strategies and gain emotional support. **TeenLine** (800-TL-TEENS) offers a confidential helpline for teens, and **TherapyRoute.com** allows you to find therapists in your area.
  - **Teen Counseling** is another great option for online therapy designed specifically for teenagers.

Community Groups and Online Resources:

- **Meetup.com** – Find local or virtual groups for teens who are interested in self-improvement, mindfulness, or building stronger relationships.
- **Reddit Subreddits** – Subreddits like r/self-improvement and r/teenagers offer a safe space to share your thoughts, seek advice, and learn from others about challenges you might face in growing up.
- **DoSomething.org** – This site encourages young people to take action in social causes, which helps build leadership skills, confidence, and a sense of purpose.
- **Girls Who Code** – For young people interested in technology, this organization helps build a community of like-minded teens who want to make a difference.
- **Teen Mentoring Programs** – Websites like **Big Brothers Big Sisters** or **iMentor**help connect teens with mentors who can provide guidance, advice, and support.

Supportive Online Courses and Platforms:

- **Skillshare** – Offers free and paid courses on creative topics such as writing, drawing, design, and personal development, helping teens tap into their creativity.
- **Coursera for Teens** – Many free online courses that teach important skills such as leadership, mindfulness, and personal growth, which can help you build confidence and a strong sense of identity.

- **Mindvalley** – Although it's for all ages, Mindvalley offers great personal development and self-help content that's accessible for teens seeking to explore their growth further.

- **Calm** and **Headspace** – These mindfulness apps offer free resources for improving focus, managing stress, and cultivating mental well-being.

Support Hotlines and Resources for Immediate Help:

- **Teen Line** (800-TL-TEENS) – A confidential helpline offering emotional support for teens dealing with stress, depression, or difficult situations.

- **Crisis Text Line**: Text HOME to 741741 (US, UK, Canada) – Provides free, 24/7 support for teens in crisis.

- **National Suicide Prevention Lifeline** (1-800-273-8255) – A free and confidential helpline for individuals facing emotional distress or suicidal thoughts.

Conclusion:

The transition from adolescence to adulthood is a crucial time for SELF-discovery, and the resources above are here to help you navigate this exciting, sometimes overwhelming, journey.

Whether you're seeking more information on how to build confidence, finding ways to develop your emotional intelligence, or looking for support when things feel tough, there's a wealth of knowledge and mentorship available to guide you.

Remember that growth is a process, and there is no need to rush it. Keep moving forward with honor, embrace who you are, and lean on the resources that help you flourish.

Made in the USA
Las Vegas, NV
05 January 2025

859b206e-a911-4b23-ac5a-7414954d6e58R01